Mel Bay and Warner Bros. Publications Prese

ROCK Goes Classic

Rock Favorites for CLASSIC GUITAR

American Pie	2
Both Sides Now	6
Brown Eyed Girl	8
City of New Orleans	11
Don't Speak	14
Europa	17
Handy Man	20
Hotel California	23
House at Pooh Corner	26
Layla	30
Lyin' Eyes	32
Margaritaville	35
Moondance	38
Nights in White Satin	41
Tears in Heaven	44
Vincent	49
Wonderful Tonight	52

The guitars on the front and back covers appear courtesy of John Buscarino.

Page 29 has been intentionally left blank.

1 2 3 4 5 6 7 8 9 0

© 2002 BY MEL BAY PUBLICATIONS, INC. AND WARNER BROS. PUBLICATIONS.
ALL RIGHTS RESERVED. INTERNATIONAL COPYRIGHT SECURED. B.M.I. MADE AND PRINTED IN U.S.A.
No part of this publication may be reproduced in whole or in part, or stored in a retrieval system, or transmitted in any form
or by any means, electronic, mechanical, photocopy, recording, or otherwise, without written permission of the publisher.

Visit us on the Web at www.melbay.com — E-mail us at email@melbay.com

American Pie

Words and Music
by Don McLean
arranged for guitar by Steve Siktberg

© 1971 Benny Bird Music. Copyright Renewed.
All Rights for Benny Bird Music Administered by Songs of Universal, Inc.

Both Sides Now

Words and Music
by Joni Mitchell
arranged for guitar by Stephen Rekas

© 1967 Siquomb Publishing Corporation.
© Renewed and Assigned to Crazy Crow Music. All Rights Reserved.

Brown Eyed Girl

Words and Music
by Van Morrison
arranged for guitar by Kirk Hanser

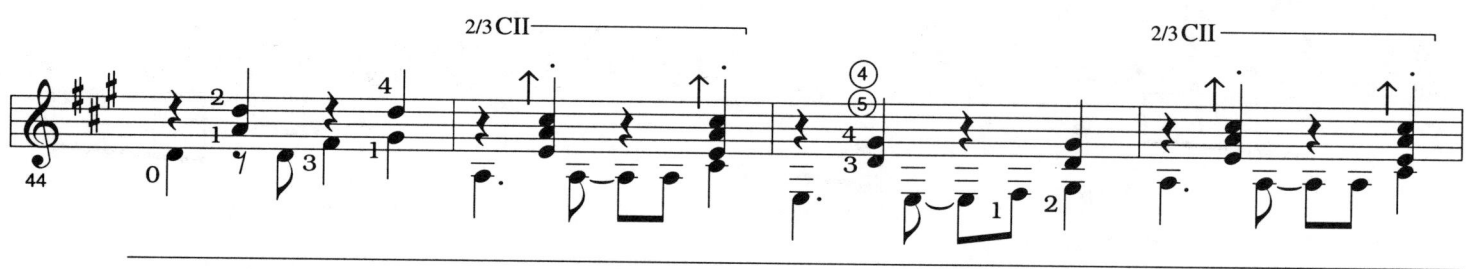
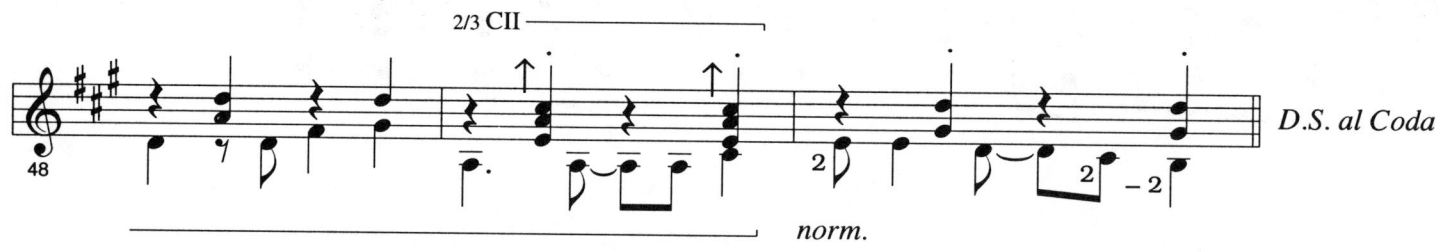

City of New Orleans

Words and Music
by Steve Goodman
arranged for guitar by Kirk Hanser

Don't Speak

*Words and Music
by Gwen Stefani and Eric Stefani
arranged for guitar by Kirk Hanser*

Europa
(Earth's Cry Heaven's Smile)

by Carlos Santana
and Tom Coster

arranged for guitar by Kirk Hanser

© 1976 Light Music (BMI). All Rights Reserved.

Handy Man

Words and Music by
Otis Blackwell and Jimmy Jones
arranged for guitar by Steve Siktberg

Hotel California

Words and Music by Don Henley,
Glenn Frey and Don Felder
arranged for guitar by Kirk Hanser

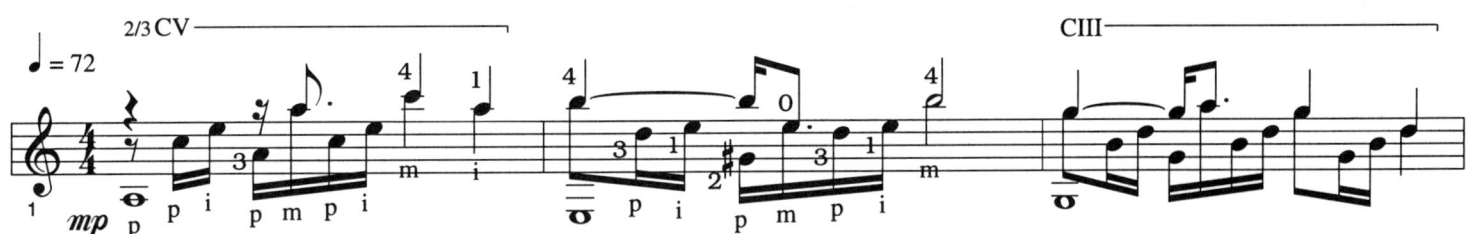

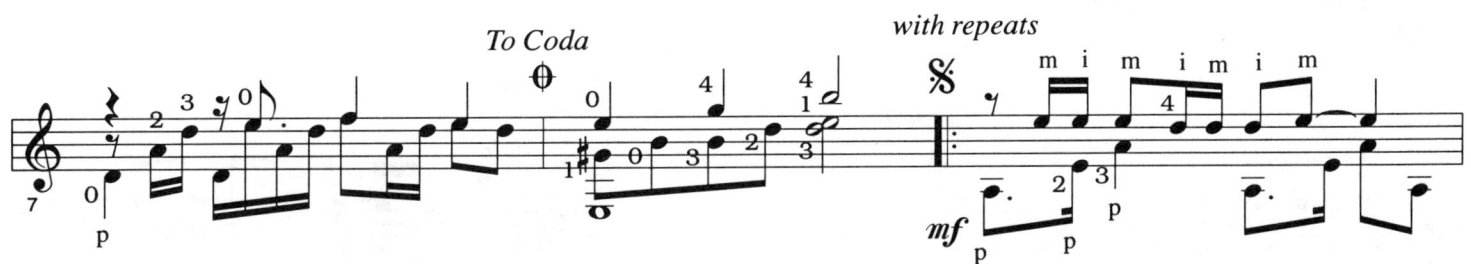

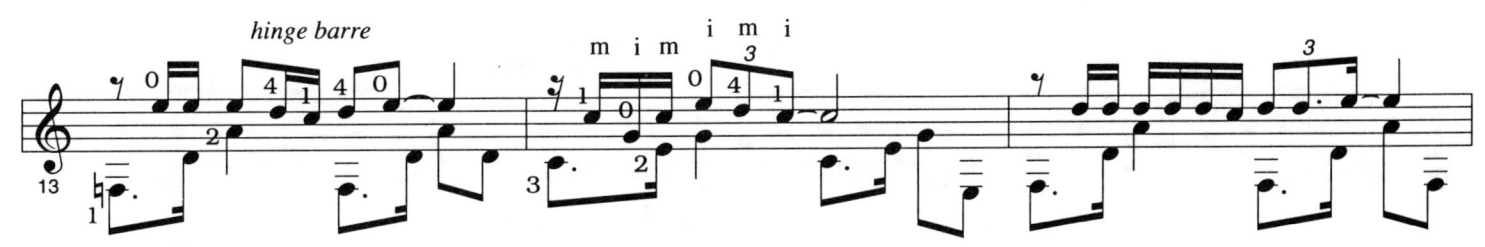

© 1976 Woody Creek Music, Red Cloud Music and Fingers Music. All Rights Reserved.

*This page has been
left blank to avoid
awkward page turns*

Layla

Words and Music by
Eric Clapton and Jim Gordon
arranged for guitar by John McClellan

♩ = 100

© 1970 Eric Patrick Clapton and Throat Music Ltd. Copyright Renewed.
All Rights Administered by Unichappell Music, Inc. All Rights Reserved.

Lyin' Eyes

Medium country rock feel ♩ = 130

Words and Music by
Don Henley and Glenn Frey
arranged for guitar by Steve Siktberg

© 1975 Woody Creek Music and Red Cloud Music. All Rights Reserved.

Margaritaville

**Words and Music
by Jimmy Buffett**
arranged for guitar by Kirk Hanser

© 1977 Coral Reefer Music. All Rights Reserved.

Moondance

**Words and Music
by Van Morrison**
arranged for guitar by Levi Dendy

♩= 132

Moderately with a swing feel

© 1970, 1971 WB Music Corporation and Caledonia Soul Music.
All Rights Administered by WB. Music Corporation.
All Rights Reserved.

Nights in White Satin

*Words and Music
by Justin Hayward
arranged for guitar by Kirk Hanser*

Tears in Heaven

**Words and Music by
Eric Clapton and Will Jennings**
arranged for guitar by Stephen Rekas

Vincent
(Starry, Starry Night)

Words and Music
by Don McLean
arranged for guitar by Kirk Hanser

© 1971 Benny Bird Music. Copyright Renewed. All Rights for Benny Bird Music Administered by Songs of Universal, Inc.
All Rights Reserved.

Wonderful Tonight

Words and Music
by Eric Clapton
arranged for guitar by Stephen Rekas

* slap fretboard lightly

© 1978 Eric Patrick Clapton. All Rights in the U.S.A. Administered by Unichappell Music Inc. All Rights Reserved.